And Now a Message from Our Corporate Lawyer:

"Neither the Publisher nor the Author shall be liable for any damage that may be caused or sustained as a result of conducting any of the activities in this book without specifically following instructions, conducting the activities without proper supervision, or ignoring the cautions contained in the book."

A TREASURE-TROVE FOR LEFTIES

Including

The Lefty Book

Hey, You There!

GIVE US A HAND!

Applause, we mean.

We'd like you to give us a big hand—a round of applause. Clap like mad, please. Right now, if you don't mind. This is a book for left-handed kids, but it's okay to use both hands to give us a round of applause.

Go ahead. *Don't be shy.*

What?? You want to know why you should applaud, especially before you've even explored this book? That's a fair question. Allow us to point out a couple applause-worthy things about *Lefty*.

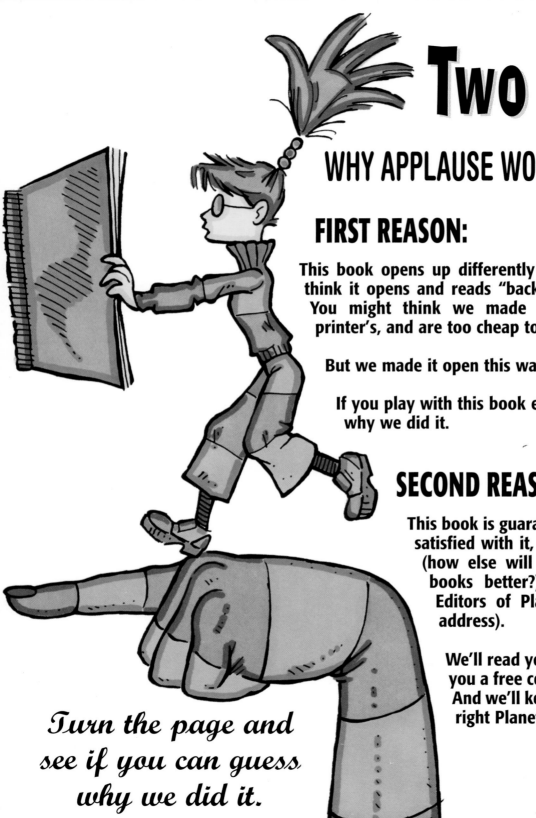

Two Reasons

WHY APPLAUSE WOULD BE APPROPRIATE:

FIRST REASON:

This book opens up differently from any other book. You might think it opens and reads "backward" (check the page numbers). You might think we made a big fat mistake at the book printer's, and are too cheap to fix it.

But we made it open this way on purpose! We're that crazy.

If you play with this book enough, you'll understand why we did it.

SECOND REASON:

This book is guaranteed! If for any reason you aren't satisfied with it, please send a note telling us why (how else will we be able to make our future books better?), along with the book, to The Editors of Planet Dexter (see page 7 for the address).

We'll read your note carefully and send back to you a free copy of another Planet Dexter book. And we'll keep doing that until we find just the right Planet Dexter book for you.

Turn the page and see if you can guess why we did it.

Top Five Reasons

TO KEEP THIS BOOK NEAR YOU AT ALL TIMES

1. It's a truly **handy** book to have around.

2. It's an informative book on the one **hand**, but on the other **hand** it's pretty strange.

3. It's a **hand**book for left-handers—a fairly rare thing.

4. It has a very **hand**some cover, which may cause your friends some envy.

5. All left-handers deserve a big **hand** for putting up with the world's right-handed books, but this one's built just for you and you might want to display it proudly.

The Editors of Planet Dexter Sinister
One Jacob Way
Reading, MA 01867-3999

True or False?

Rumor has it that left-handed people are more "playful" and more "psychic" than right-handed people. We don't know if this is true, but if you're left-handed, we'd love for you to write to us and tell us whether you agree.

We'd like to hear what you think of this book, too. Tell us about it in your "playful" manner. Of course, if you're really "psychic," we won't have to give you our address—you'll just know it. But in case you're not, write to us at the address on the left.

Or fax us at (617) 944-8243. Or zap us via the Internet at pdexter@awl.com.

We'll do our best to write back to you as soon as we can. You'll know our envelope when it arrives. We almost always put our return address in the upper left-hand corner.

No Admittance Beyond this Point

UNLESS YOU'RE LEFT-HANDED, OR CAN AT LEAST FAKE IT

Aaaaaaaaa! It's the Beatles!! The Fab Four!!

Notice anything . . . funny about them?

Besides their hair and the way Paul's staring at the ceiling, that is?

Here's a hint: two of them are left-handed. Can you tell which two?

The answer's printed at the bottom of this page.

If two out of the four Beatles were left-handed, that means that half of the Beatles were left-handed, which is an awful lot. In the Beatles, being left-handed is just as common as being right-handed. But in the population of the whole world, it's pretty rare to be left-handed.

In fact, out of every ten people you meet, less than two will be left-handed. Not a lot. But, somehow, many famous people manage to be left-handed. Go figure.

Turn the page to find a list of famous people who would like to read this book. In each row, one is left-handed, and one is not. Please guess which one in each row, being a left-hander, should be allowed to read the rest of this book, and which one, being a right-hander, should be forced to wait here, on pages 8 and 9, unless he or she can learn to at least fake being a left-hander for the next 55 pages.

THE LEFTY TYPE

Whenever you type, your left hand does more than half (60 percent) of the work because most of the more popular letters (a, e, r, s, t) are on the left side of the keyboard.

8

Answers: Ringo Starr (drums) and Paul McCartney (far left) are the left-handers. You can tell Paul is left-handed because he holds his guitar left-handedly.

9

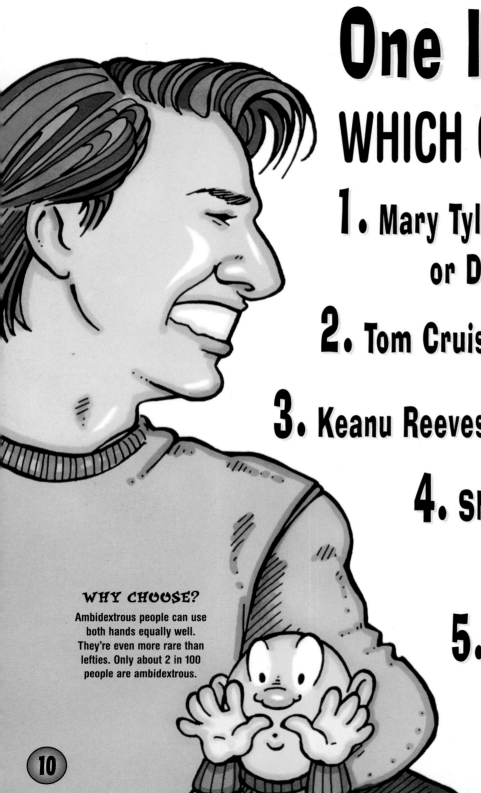

One Is, One Isn't.
WHICH ONE IS?

1. Mary Tyler Moore
or Dick Van Dyke?

2. Tom Cruise or Brad Pitt?

3. Keanu Reeves or Michael J. Fox?

4. Sharon Stone
or Nicole Kidman?

5. Julia Roberts
or Jonathan Taylor Thomas?

WHY CHOOSE?
Ambidextrous people can use both hands equally well. They're even more rare than lefties. Only about 2 in 100 people are ambidextrous.

10

6. Mary-Kate Olsen

or Ashley Olsen?

7. Wilma Flintstone

or Bart Simpson?

8. Miss Piggy or Kermit the Frog?

9. Oprah Winfrey

or Rosie O'Donnell?

10. Bill Clinton

or Hillary Clinton?

HAND TEST
Quick. Fold your hands. Which thumb lies on top? Bet it's the right one, if you're a lefty.

Answers are on page 60.

We Interrupt this Program

TO BRING YOU A LITTLE COMMERCIAL FOR B.F.

Can you read this? It's said that left-handers are more talented than right-handers at reading words printed backwards and read right to left. Seems pretty cool, if it's true, because then left-handers can have their own secret code. If it starts giving you a headache to read this way, hey, what can we say? We're Planet Sinister!

Anyhow, this page is dedicated to Benjamin Franklin (1706–1790). Yep, the guy who discovered that lightning was made of electricity by flying a kite with a key tied to it during a big storm. Ben Franklin was left-handed, and one of the many nifty things he accomplished in life was the creation of the first lending library. He thought it would be great if people too poor to buy books could still borrow and read them. He also owned his own printing press for a while, and printed newspapers that had comics and pictures in them. Ben Franklin wanted everyone to read. So what you're doing right now would make him happy.

BACK TO THE FUTURE
As a left-handed kid, Paul McCartney of the Beatles used to try to peddle his bike backwards.

Just thought we'd mention that.

COLD HANDS,
WARM HEART
There's a place in Alaska
called Lefthand Bay.

13

How to Spot a Lefty

PART I (BABIES)

Some people are bird-watchers, some people are people-watchers. Here's how to start to become a left-hander-watcher. Watch some babies.

Little Suckers

Even before babies are born, parents can get a clue about whether that kid's going to grow up to be a lefty or a righty. Scientists think that you can tell during ultrasound exams (when doctors use sound waves and complicated equipment to show parents what the baby's up to while it's still inside mom). Often during ultrasounds, the little unborn baby is seen sucking his or her unborn thumb. Babies who will be left-handed tend to suck the left thumb (what else is there to do in there?), and babies who will be right-handed prefer the right thumb.

One psychologist looked at ultrasounds of 224 babies, and found that only 12 of them sucked the left thumb. **That sucks.**

The Head Clue

Left-handed babies tend to look to the left just after they're born, whereas right-handed babies prefer to look to the right.

Twin Thing

Identical twins—the kind who look almost exactly alike—have exactly the same genes, so you would think that if one twin is a left-hander, the other one would be, too. But no, not always. Look at the famous Olsen twins: Mary-Kate is, Ashley isn't. Some people think that twins are sometimes so crowded together in their mom's body before they're born that they have to develop different handedness so they're not always bumping into each other.

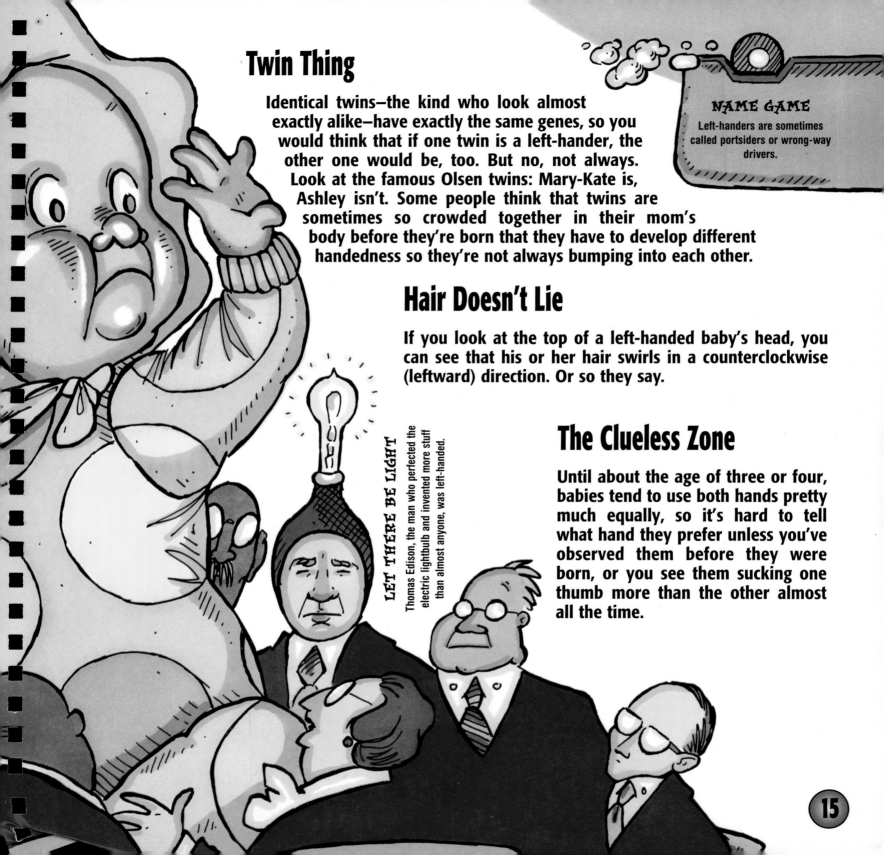

NAME GAME

Left-handers are sometimes called portsiders or wrong-way drivers.

Hair Doesn't Lie

If you look at the top of a left-handed baby's head, you can see that his or her hair swirls in a counterclockwise (leftward) direction. Or so they say.

LET THERE BE LIGHT

Thomas Edison, the man who perfected the electric lightbulb and invented more stuff than almost anyone, was left-handed.

The Clueless Zone

Until about the age of three or four, babies tend to use both hands pretty much equally, so it's hard to tell what hand they prefer unless you've observed them before they were born, or you see them sucking one thumb more than the other almost all the time.

15

How to Spot a Lefty,
PART II (DEAD AND ANCIENT PEOPLE)

Do you know how to tell whether someone who is no longer alive was right-handed or left-handed? Can you imagine a situation in which you would actually care?

Never mind. Take our quiz to test yourself.

1. You wake up one fine autumn morning and find a fully preserved Egyptian mummy lying on the grass outside your bedroom window. The first thing you think is, "Gee, I wonder if he or she was left-handed, like me?" So you:

a. offer the mummy a Bic and a pad of paper, and ask for his or her autograph.

b. tickle the mummy and hope that he or she will push you away with his or her dominant hand.

c. get a tape measure from the garage and measure to see which of the mummy's arms is longer.

2. On your way to school, still puzzling over the fully preserved Egyptian mummy, you almost stumble over a suit of armor lying across your neighbor's sidewalk. To find out if the armor belonged to a left- or right-handed person, you:

a. knock on the chest and call out, "Yoo-hoo! Anybody *left* in this thing?"

b. check to see if the suit of armor includes a shoulder shield, and if so, what side it's on.

c. show the suit of armor this book and see if it looks a little excited.

3. On your way home from school that night, you notice a cave you've never seen before, right behind the Dunkin' Donuts. The cave is empty but it's full of stuff left by some long-dead cave person. In order to figure out if that cave person was right-handed or left-handed, you:

a. sniff around for some *left*-overs.

b. check to see if you can find any tools the cave people might have used, and then look to see if any of those tools are sharpened on the right side.

c. check to see if you can find any cave graffiti that reads, "Lefties rule the cave."

TECHNO WIZARDS

If it weren't for lefties, we wouldn't have the Macintosh computer. Out of the five people who designed it, four were left-handed.

SMELLS LIKE TEEN LEFTINESS

Kurt Cobain, of Nirvana, was a left-hander.

17

How to Spot a Lefty, Part III

FAMOUS LEFTIES — A FORBIDDEN MATCHING GAME

You've probably been told a million times that it isn't nice to "stereotype" people. And it isn't! People are never just one thing, and it's pretty uncool to reduce them to a "type."

That said, however, why don't you see if you can match the following left-handers with the following high school cliques. For example, if Whoopi Goldberg were in high school, would she be in Marching Band, or a Class Clown? You should be able to put two famous left-handers into each clique.

See if your calls jibe with ours, which can be found on page 60.

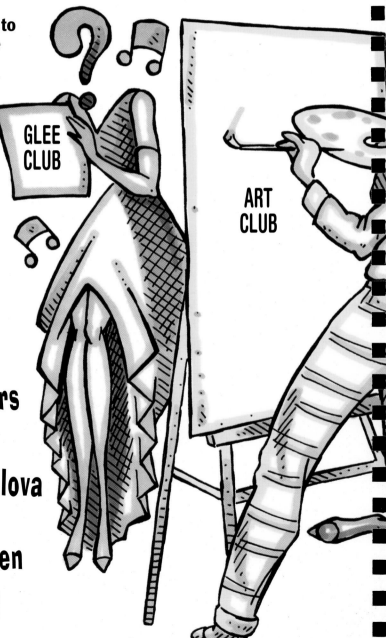

FAMOUS LEFTIES

Whoopi Goldberg

Jay Leno

Pablo Picasso

Michael Stipe of REM

George Bush

Julia Roberts

H. Ross Perot

Marilyn Monroe

"Neon" Deion Sanders

Jimi Hendrix

Martina Navratilova

Judy Garland

Ludwig van Beethoven

Leonardo da Vinci

18

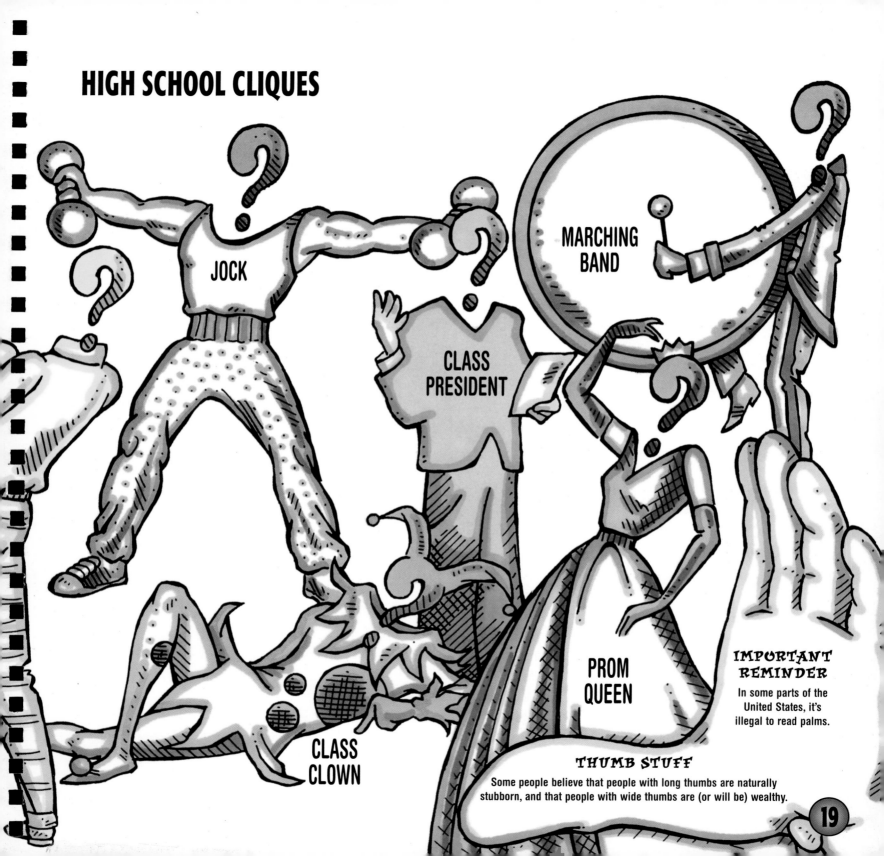

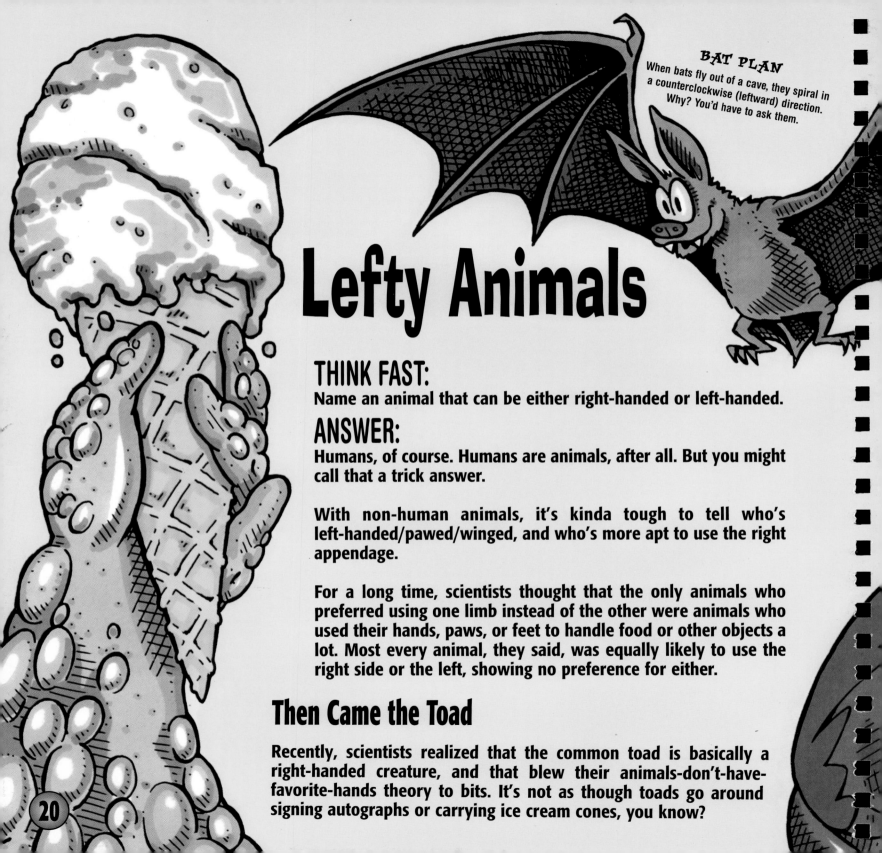

Lefty Animals

THINK FAST:

Name an animal that can be either right-handed or left-handed.

ANSWER:

Humans, of course. Humans are animals, after all. But you might call that a trick answer.

With non-human animals, it's kinda tough to tell who's left-handed/pawed/winged, and who's more apt to use the right appendage.

For a long time, scientists thought that the only animals who preferred using one limb instead of the other were animals who used their hands, paws, or feet to handle food or other objects a lot. Most every animal, they said, was equally likely to use the right side or the left, showing no preference for either.

Then Came the Toad

Recently, scientists realized that the common toad is basically a right-handed creature, and that blew their animals-don't-have-favorite-hands theory to bits. It's not as though toads go around signing autographs or carrying ice cream cones, you know?

Some other animals who show a fondness for the left side are:

• Cats, rats, and mice.

It's not really nice of us to lump together cats, rats, and mice, but it's a fact that all these animals are equally as likely to be left-pawed as right-pawed.

• Primates.

Some ape-like animals, such as lemurs (LEE-murs) and galagos (geh-LAH-gos), also known as bush babies, are generally left-handed. Research in zoos showed that they like to use their left hands to fetch food out of the moats around their enclosures.

• Lobsters.

You can tell whether a lobster is right-clawed or left-clawed by looking to see which claw is the largest (left-clawed lobsters have larger left claws).

• Parrots.

Yep. Parrots seem to be left-footed most of the time. Given a choice between picking up an cracker with the left foot or the right, Polly usually chooses the left.

TOOTH TWIRL

Arctic whales, called "narwhals" (NAR-walls), grow long tusks that curl into a spiral in a counterclockwise (leftward) direction.

21

Spot the Lefty:
THE ULTIMATE CHALLENGE

How many lefties are in this picture?

Our count, and our answers, are on page 60.

CAUGHT RED HANDED

When you see a red wax seal on the back of a letter, try to remember that once upon a time, people did this kind of letter-sealing with a bloody hand! Seriously. It was considered a seal of authority.

I SWEAR

People who are swearing to something (like in court) often raise their right hands first. But a long time ago, instead of doing that, they'd simply say, "I will put my hand in the fire and it will not burn!" People are strange.

23

How to Make a Lefty
A MAD SCIENTIST'S NOTES

Guess what.

No one yet knows why some people are left-handed and some are right-handed. Many scientists have worried over this question, but they're still basically clueless.

Below, you'll find some of the theories put forth by real scientists today, theories that many people take seriously, and also a couple of theories so weird that they could only be the ideas of truly "mad" scientists.

We'll tip you off to phony theories on page 61.

The Boy Hormone Theory

When a woman is pregnant, she sometimes has a little extra testosterone (a male hormone, or body chemical) in her system. One theory holds that the extra testosterone causes the baby to become left-handed. People who believe this say that one of the reasons it might make sense is because there are more than twice as many left-handed boys than left-handed girls. And boy babies are more likely to generate extra testosterone.

The Smelly Theory

If a woman or man carrying a newborn baby around town encounters lots of strong odors—car exhaust fumes, colognes, b.o.—the baby begins to hold her right hand in an attempt to protect her nose, and thus becomes more adept at gesturing and manipulating objects with her left hand.

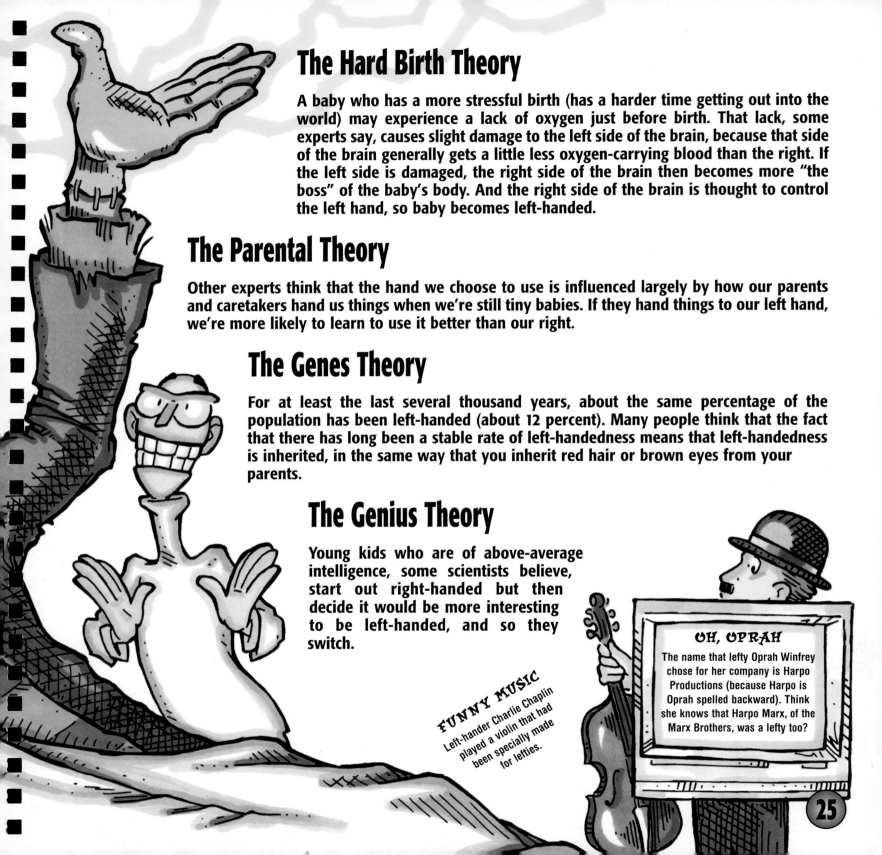

The Hard Birth Theory

A baby who has a more stressful birth (has a harder time getting out into the world) may experience a lack of oxygen just before birth. That lack, some experts say, causes slight damage to the left side of the brain, because that side of the brain generally gets a little less oxygen-carrying blood than the right. If the left side is damaged, the right side of the brain then becomes more "the boss" of the baby's body. And the right side of the brain is thought to control the left hand, so baby becomes left-handed.

The Parental Theory

Other experts think that the hand we choose to use is influenced largely by how our parents and caretakers hand us things when we're still tiny babies. If they hand things to our left hand, we're more likely to learn to use it better than our right.

The Genes Theory

For at least the last several thousand years, about the same percentage of the population has been left-handed (about 12 percent). Many people think that the fact that there has long been a stable rate of left-handedness means that left-handedness is inherited, in the same way that you inherit red hair or brown eyes from your parents.

The Genius Theory

Young kids who are of above-average intelligence, some scientists believe, start out right-handed but then decide it would be more interesting to be left-handed, and so they switch.

FUNNY MUSIC

Left-hander Charlie Chaplin played a violin that had been specially made for lefties.

OH, OPRAH

The name that lefty Oprah Winfrey chose for her company is Harpo Productions (because Harpo is Oprah spelled backward). Think she knows that Harpo Marx, of the Marx Brothers, was a lefty too?

Brain Lies

UNTRUE STUFF THAT MOST PEOPLE BELIEVE

You've probably heard the saying, "If the right side of the body is controlled by the left side of the brain, and the left side of the body is controlled by the right side of the brain, left-handers are the only people in their right minds."

That saying is based on the fact that the brain has two halves—the right half and the left half. But beware. There are lots of myths about the brain's two halves.

What Folks Say

The right side of the body is controlled by the left side of the brain, and the left side of the body is controlled by the right side of the brain. Therefore, left-handers are "right brain dominant" (ruled more by the right side of their brain than the left). Because the right side of the brain thinks in pictures, whereas the left side thinks in words, left-handers are less talented at writing and speaking, and more talented at stuff like music and art.

What's True

Scientists have been unable to find evidence that lefties are necessarily more right-brained (artistic, dreamy, musical) and righties are necessarily more left-brained (logical, talkative, responsible).

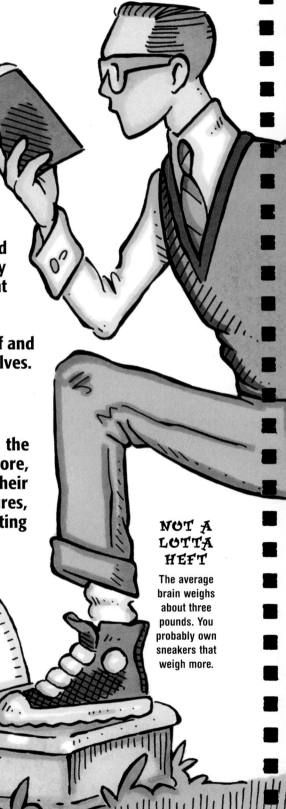

NOT A LOTTA HEFT

The average brain weighs about three pounds. You probably own sneakers that weigh more.

What Folks Say

The brains of left-handers are different from the brains of right-handers because in left-handers the right side of the brain does most of the work.

What's True

The main difference between the brain of a right-hander and the brain of a left-hander seems to be that the corpus callosum (COR-pus cal-OH-sum) in lefties (and in ambidextrous people) is bigger than it is in righties. What's the corpus collosum? It's the part of the brain that connects the right and left halves of the brain and sends information between the two parts. So left-handers have brains whose halves are more likely to work together on tasks.

What Folks Say

If you want to cut into the brain of a left-hander and not damage his ability to speak, you're safe cutting into the left half of the brain.

What's True

The language part of a left-hander's brain can be located on either side in a left-hander, or even on both sides. So you'd better not cut into the brain at all, okay?

LEFTIES ARE NERVIER?
The corpus collosum in the brain of a left-hander or ambidextrous person may have 25 million more nerve fibers than the corpus collosum in the brain of a right-hander.

BEST FOOT FORWARD
"Goofy-footed" is the slang term for someone who skateboards left-footed.

Lefties Under the Microscope

WHAT THE EXPERTS ARE REPORTING ABOUT YOU

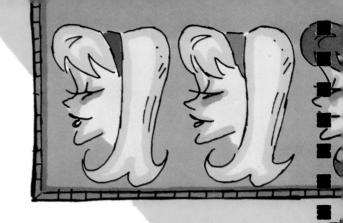

Leftier and Smarter?

Left-handed female college students are better than right-handed female college students at geography, according to some researchers. Gotta wonder how much money they spent to find that out.

The Twins

Identical twins have identical genes. But for some reason even identical twins are no more likely to both be left- or right-handed than are any other pairs of siblings.

You and your brother or sister are only a little bit more likely to have the same handedness as are any two complete strangers.

Left Out

A survey of scientific data over many decades showed that even if both of your parents are left-handed, you are more than twice as likely to be born a right-handed child than a left-handed one. Lefties are that rare.

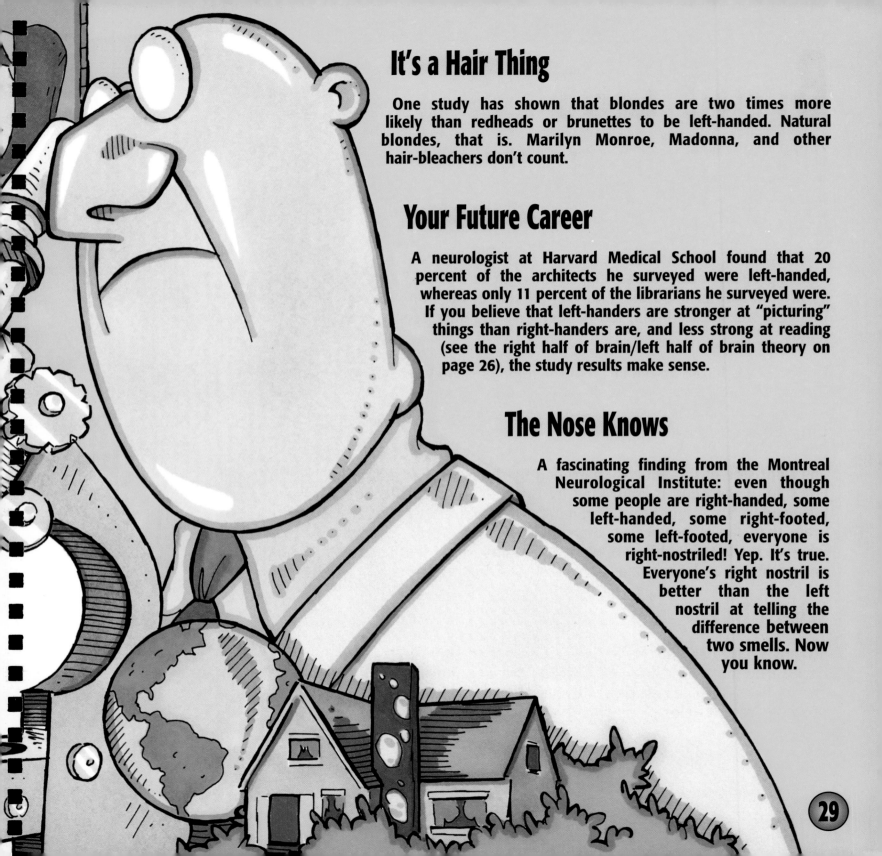

It's a Hair Thing

One study has shown that blondes are two times more likely than redheads or brunettes to be left-handed. Natural blondes, that is. Marilyn Monroe, Madonna, and other hair-bleachers don't count.

Your Future Career

A neurologist at Harvard Medical School found that 20 percent of the architects he surveyed were left-handed, whereas only 11 percent of the librarians he surveyed were. If you believe that left-handers are stronger at "picturing" things than right-handers are, and less strong at reading (see the right half of brain/left half of brain theory on page 26), the study results make sense.

The Nose Knows

A fascinating finding from the Montreal Neurological Institute: even though some people are right-handed, some left-handed, some right-footed, some left-footed, everyone is right-nostriled! Yep. It's true. Everyone's right nostril is better than the left nostril at telling the difference between two smells. Now you know.

Are You the Next Albert Einstein?

A NO-BRAINER WAY TO TELL

Page 29 of this book mentions a nostril study. Did you read that and go, **"No way!"**?

Well, you'll just have to take our word for it. We can't think of how to prove that to you. Instead, we're going to show you a little test you can give yourself to determine if you are right-eyed or left-eyed.

There's something we should mention first. If you find that you are right-eyed yet left-handed, or left-eyed yet right-handed, it's time for you to run around like a hyper spazz for a minute or two. Why? Because you're possibly much more hugely talented than you ever expected!

Albert Einstein wrote with his right hand, but looked through telescopes with his left eye, for instance, which probably means that he was "cross-dominant" (the term for someone who is left-eyed and right-handed, or the other way around). And look how special and smart people consider him!

Cross-dominant people are said to be more creative than the rest of us.

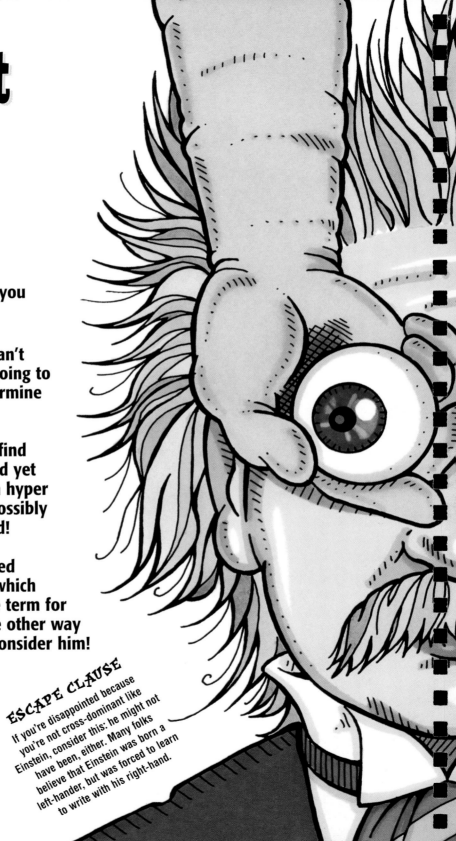

ESCAPE CLAUSE

If you're disappointed because you're not cross-dominant like Einstein, consider this: he might not have been, either. Many folks believe that Einstein was born a left-hander, but was forced to learn to write with his right-hand.

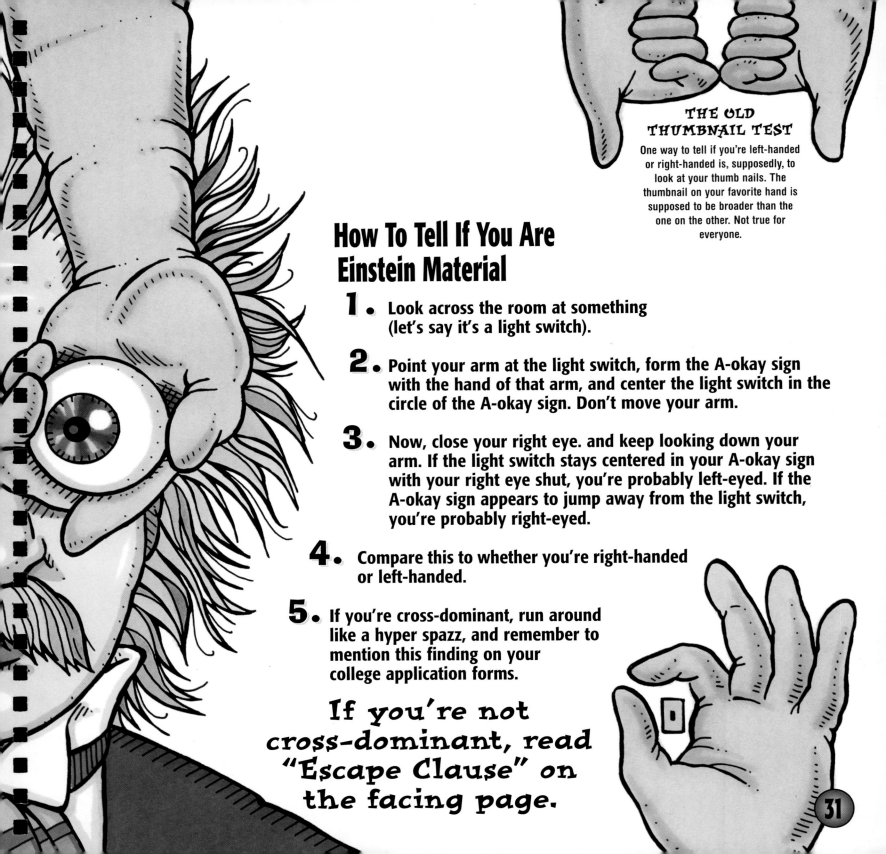

How To Tell If You Are Einstein Material

1. Look across the room at something (let's say it's a light switch).

2. Point your arm at the light switch, form the A-okay sign with the hand of that arm, and center the light switch in the circle of the A-okay sign. Don't move your arm.

3. Now, close your right eye. and keep looking down your arm. If the light switch stays centered in your A-okay sign with your right eye shut, you're probably left-eyed. If the A-okay sign appears to jump away from the light switch, you're probably right-eyed.

4. Compare this to whether you're right-handed or left-handed.

5. If you're cross-dominant, run around like a hyper spazz, and remember to mention this finding on your college application forms.

If you're not cross-dominant, read "Escape Clause" on the facing page.

Somewhere,
LEFT OF THE RAINBOW

Judy Garland was a left-hander. Think about what that means. More people have seen "The Wizard of Oz" than any other movie in the history of the world. Thus, Judy is perhaps the most famous movie star ever. (And Toto is the most famous movie dog.)

Being left-handed doesn't seem to have changed Judy Garland's life much. She was one busy mama, that's for sure. She starred in 43 movies, was featured on more than 200 radio shows, and performed in at least 1,100 concert and nightclub gigs. If you go to a really good record store, you can choose from over 100 Judy Garland albums.

It's kinda cool to watch Judy in "The Wizard of Oz" once you know she's a lefty. You'll notice that she carries her basket on her left arm most of the time.

TALENTED LADY

Judy Garland wrote with her left hand, and described herself as a left-hander, but by some accounts, she used her right hand when she drew pictures.

A little tip from a big star:

"When I write," Judy once explained, "my hand smudges the ink as I cross the page. I've discovered that putting talcum powder on my hand will permit it to ride along without smudging."

CHEAP THRILLS

When Judy Garland and her sisters were very young, they put on back-yard shows for their neighbors. Admission price: 10 straight pins (the kind you use for sewing). Good thing she finally got an agent.

When Lefties Ruled the World

AT LEAST KINDA (FILL IN THE BLANKS)

1. Back in Stone Age times, it's very possible that left-handers were _____ .

    a. stronger than right-handers, and won all the arm-wresting contests hands down
    b. in a pretty bad mood, due to the lack of TV
    c. just as numerous as right-handers
    d. worshipped as if they were holy

2. Archeologists count prehistoric left-handers by examining cave walls for _____ .

    a. drawings of animals and people whose profiles face to the right
    b. lefty thumb-prints
    c. signatures that look as though they were made with the left hand
    d. sneeze marks that indicate a leftward spray

3. It's possible that before the Bronze Age (3,000 to 1,000 B.C.), half of the people were left-handed, and half were right-handed. _____ is thought to have reduced the number of left-handers dramatically.

    a. The invention of the wheel
    b. A really bad flu
    c. A big, hairy right-handed bully
    d. The invention of bronze tools

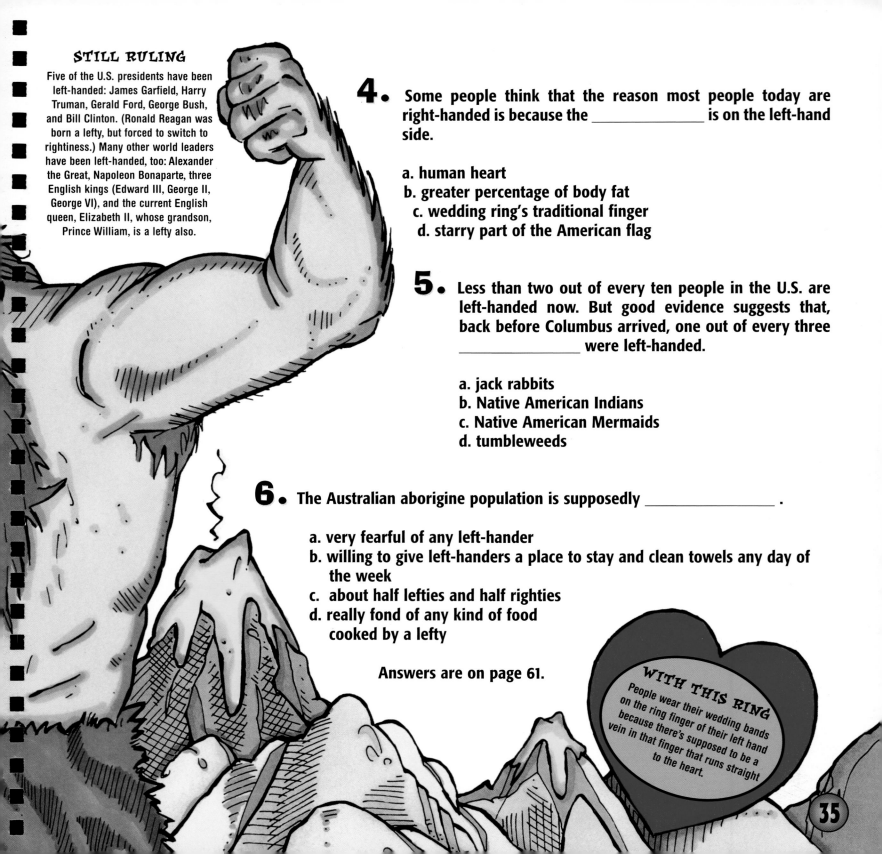

STILL RULING

Five of the U.S. presidents have been left-handed: James Garfield, Harry Truman, Gerald Ford, George Bush, and Bill Clinton. (Ronald Reagan was born a lefty, but forced to switch to rightiness.) Many other world leaders have been left-handed, too: Alexander the Great, Napoleon Bonaparte, three English kings (Edward III, George II, George VI), and the current English queen, Elizabeth II, whose grandson, Prince William, is a lefty also.

4. Some people think that the reason most people today are right-handed is because the _____ is on the left-hand side.

a. human heart
b. greater percentage of body fat
c. wedding ring's traditional finger
d. starry part of the American flag

5. Less than two out of every ten people in the U.S. are left-handed now. But good evidence suggests that, back before Columbus arrived, one out of every three _____ were left-handed.

a. jack rabbits
b. Native American Indians
c. Native American Mermaids
d. tumbleweeds

6. The Australian aborigine population is supposedly _____ .

a. very fearful of any left-hander
b. willing to give left-handers a place to stay and clean towels any day of the week
c. about half lefties and half righties
d. really fond of any kind of food cooked by a lefty

Answers are on page 61.

WITH THIS RING
People wear their wedding bands on the ring finger of their left hand because there's supposed to be a vein in that finger that runs straight to the heart.

Weird about Hands

SUPERSTITIONS GALORE

Have you reached the point in this book where you ask yourself, "Hey: What am I doing reading a whole book about hand stuff? Do I need to get a life?"

If so, the answer is, No, you don't need to get a life. You already have one. And you're not the only person to be interested in hands. People have been weird about hands for thousands of years. If you don't believe it, take our Weird about Hands test.

1. An itching thumb was once thought to be a sign that the person with the itchy thumb was:
   - a. not very clean.
   - b. going to hitchhike before the week was over.
   - c. going to have a visitor soon.
   - d. going to be the next Siskel or Ebert.

2. In the Middle Ages, people thought it was very lucky to own:
   - a. the hand of a broken clock.
   - b. the hand of a hanged man.
   - c. the hand of a genuine troll.
   - d. the hand of a monkey.

3. Also in the Middle Ages (apparently a pretty bizarre time to be alive), people believed you could overpower a witch if you:
   - a. happened to be a bigger witch yourself.
   - b. threw water on her, like Dorothy did.
   - c. handed her a raisin dipped in worm poison.
   - d. hit her with your left hand.

4. An old Irish saying claims that if you want milk to turn to cream more quickly you should:
   - a. hand-feed your cows lots of Redi-Whip.
   - b. use your left hand to milk the cow.
   - c. hand the milk container to someone who knows what he or she's doing.
   - d. dip the hand of a dead man into a pail of the milk.

5. The Theddora and Ngarigo societies of southeastern Australia ate the hands of their enemies after killing them because:
    a. they really liked handwiches.
    b. they thought that by eating the hands they'd be given the skills and bravery of the dead enemies.
    c. they couldn't think of anything else to do with them.
    d. they thought that if they didn't eat the hands, the enemies would rise up from their graves and strangle them.

6. Many people have believed that if your left palm itches:
    a. you're going to lose money soon.
    b. you should scratch it.
    c. you should stop using it to put itching powder in your sister's friends' sleeping bags.
    d. you're going to win the lottery.

7. At one time, people believed that if someone had magic powers, the powers could be found in:
    a. a top hat.
    b. a theater near you.
    c. a Duracell battery.
    d. a person's hands.

The answers can be found on page 61, of course.

INSURANCE

LIE DETECTOR

A magazine article about how to hire honest insurance agents featured the following information: you can tell whether a person is telling the truth by watching that person's eyes while you talk to him. If, when answering a question, he looks to the left, he's remembering facts, and is therefore telling the truth. If, when answering a question, he looks to the right, he's thinking about the future, or how things could be, or maybe a lie. The article said that the above advice was for evaluating right-handed people. The opposite would be true for lefties.

Sounds pretty bogus. But you might want to remember it if you ever need to lie during an interview at an insurance agency.

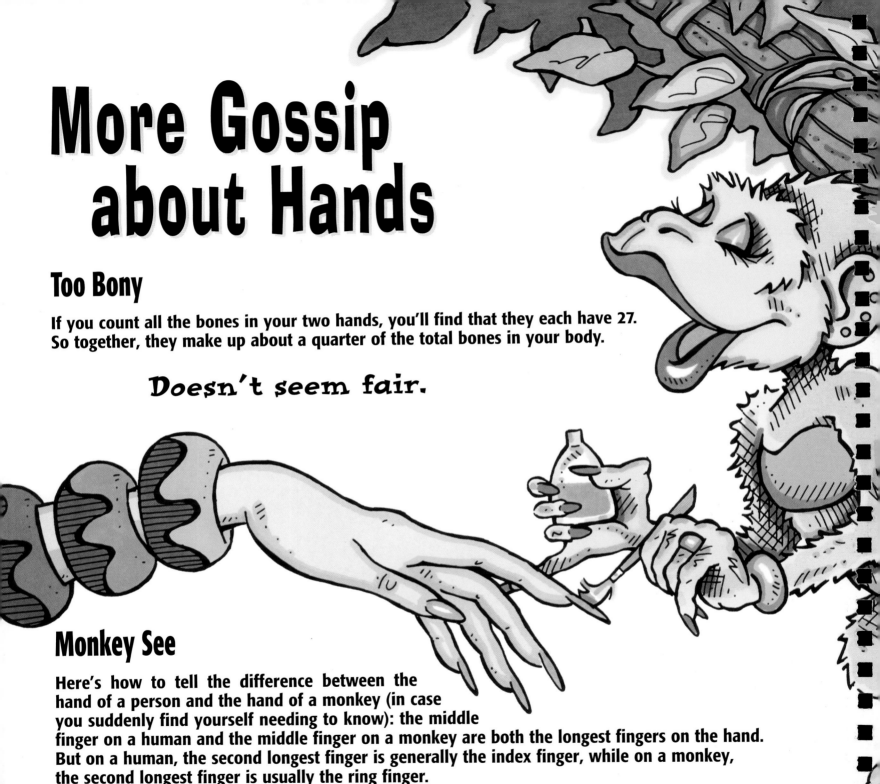

More Gossip about Hands

Too Bony

If you count all the bones in your two hands, you'll find that they each have 27. So together, they make up about a quarter of the total bones in your body.

Doesn't seem fair.

Monkey See

Here's how to tell the difference between the hand of a person and the hand of a monkey (in case you suddenly find yourself needing to know): the middle finger on a human and the middle finger on a monkey are both the longest fingers on the hand. But on a human, the second longest finger is generally the index finger, while on a monkey, the second longest finger is usually the ring finger.

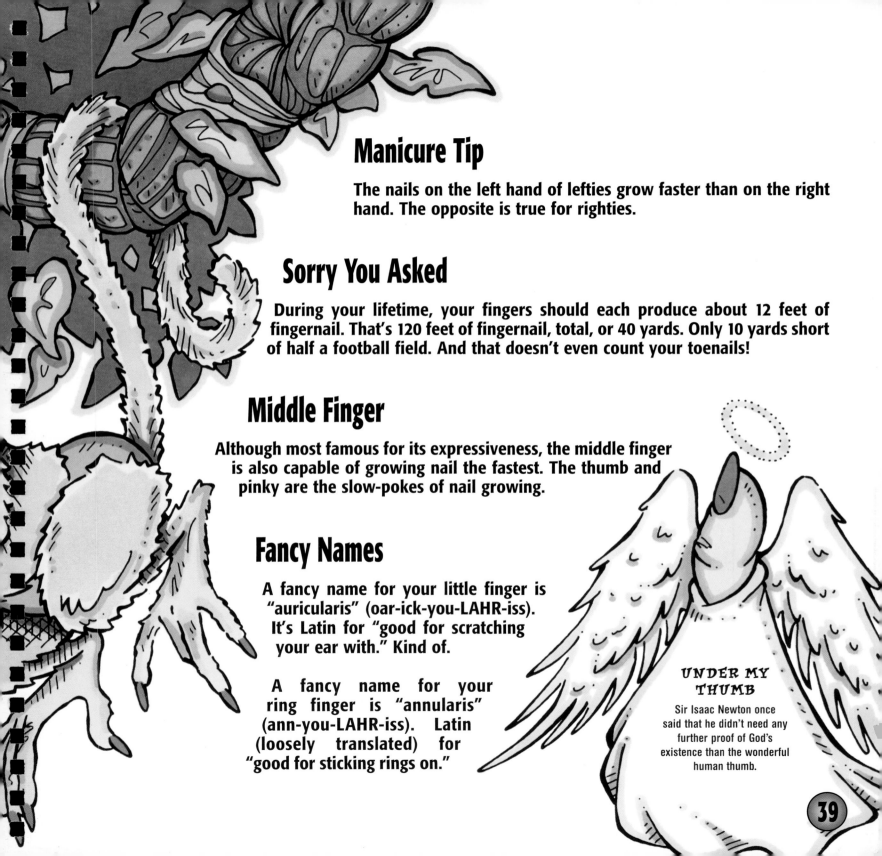

Manicure Tip

The nails on the left hand of lefties grow faster than on the right hand. The opposite is true for righties.

Sorry You Asked

During your lifetime, your fingers should each produce about 12 feet of fingernail. That's 120 feet of fingernail, total, or 40 yards. Only 10 yards short of half a football field. And that doesn't even count your toenails!

Middle Finger

Although most famous for its expressiveness, the middle finger is also capable of growing nail the fastest. The thumb and pinky are the slow-pokes of nail growing.

Fancy Names

A fancy name for your little finger is "auricularis" (oar-ick-you-LAHR-iss). It's Latin for "good for scratching your ear with." Kind of.

A fancy name for your ring finger is "annularis" (ann-you-LAHR-iss). Latin (loosely translated) for "good for sticking rings on."

UNDER MY THUMB

Sir Isaac Newton once said that he didn't need any further proof of God's existence than the wonderful human thumb.

39

Oh, No!

IT'S THE BUMMER PAGES!

These two pages are totally polluted by ugly, bad, and almost always untrue things that people have said and/or believed about left-handers over time. It makes the blood boil.

Can you find the fake bummers?

See page 61 for details a.s.a.p.

"**L**eft-handers are more stubborn than right-handers."

"**L**eft-handers have a serious body odor problem."

"**L**eft-handers are really good at cracking safes, but they're such bad luck that they always get caught."

"**L**eft-handers are an embarrassment to their families."

"**L**eft-handers are more likely than right-handers to spend money on useless appliances."

"**L**eft-handers have speech problems."

"**L**eft-handers are more likely than right-handers to get migraine headaches."

"**L**eft-handers are antisocial."

"**L**eft-handers are clumsy."

"**L**eft-handers are more likely than right-handers to end up in an emergency room."

"**L**eft-handers are more likely than right-handers to buy shoes in the wrong size."

"**L**eft-handers are more likely than right-handers to have allergies."

MAY THE FORCE BE WITH YOU

Mark Hamill, the actor who played Luke Skywalker in the "Star Wars" movies, is a lefty.

COLD COMFORT

Lefty Ludwig van Beethoven would sometimes pour ice water on his head when he was composing. He thought that doing so would make his brain work better.

God Bless Baseball

THE NYA-NYA-NYA-NYA-*NYA*-NYA PAGES

Lefties kick butt at baseball. It's a fact that no righty can dispute. If you did a little survey of the players at a professional baseball game, you would probably find that there are twice as many lefties on the field (percentage-wise) than lefties in the stadium watching. And that doesn't even count the right-handed players who are so impressed with lefty players' skills that they play left-handed themselves.

Why lefties are excellent at baseball:

- When batting, lefties stand on the first-base side of home plate, a different position than righties, which gives them about a four-foot head start to first base.

- When pitching, a lefty's throws "curve" or "move" more, so it's harder for a right-handed batter to predict where the ball will be when it crosses the plate. Of course, the same is true when a righty pitches to a lefty batter. But since most batters are righties, lefty pitchers are highly valued.

- When pitching, a lefty can keep an eye on the first-base runner so he doesn't steal second base.

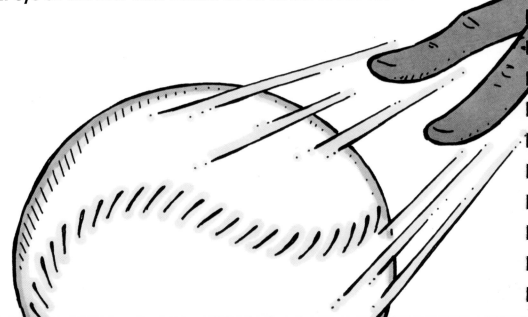

THERE'S A DAY FOR US

Every August 13 is International Left-Handers Day.

TEST YOUR BASEBALL SMARTS

Match the Baseball Player with his Achievement

1. Ted Williams
2. Reggie Jackson
3. Babe Ruth
4. Sandy Koufax
5. Ty Cobb
6. Lou Gehrig
7. Ricky Henderson
8. Tony Gwynn
9. Ken Griffey, Jr.

a. Played 2,130 consecutive games between 1925 and 1939
b. Held record for stealing home plate—35 times
c. Was considered the best hitter of his era
d. Nicknamed "The Man with the Golden Arm"
e. Hit five home runs in the 1977 World Series
f. Had best home run average, ever
g. Holds the record for most consecutive games (8) hitting one or more home runs
h. Has stolen more bases than anyone who has ever played the game
i. Has won the National League batting championship six times

1.c; 2.e; 3.f; 4.d; 5.b; 6.a; 7.h; 8.i; 9.g.

43

More Nya-Nyas

LEFTY SUPERIORITY

Not Spastic

Some people say that left-handers have poorer handwriting than righties, but that's a bunch of hooey. In fact, many lefties are especially gifted at artistic tasks, drawing especially. The guy who draws Bart Simpson is a lefty, as is the woman who draws the "Cathy" cartoon strip. At one point the owner of the Fleisher Studios in Miami, Florida, which made cartoons, had a staff of 700 cartoonists, and more than half of them were lefties.

More Adaptable

Maybe because lefties have to use so much stuff designed for righties, they're naturally better at using both hands than are righties. It's believed that the great artist Michelangelo was either left-handed or ambidextrous. While painting the Sistine Chapel, he was able to let his hands take turns painting. That way, each hand got to kick back and relax now and then.

I See You

Lefties are said to be better at seeing underwater than are righties. Could it be a coincidence that Peter Benchley, the author of "Jaws," is a left-hander?

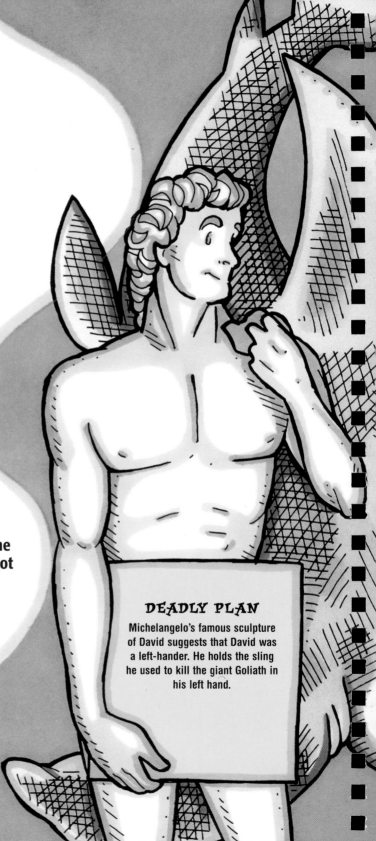

DEADLY PLAN

Michelangelo's famous sculpture of David suggests that David was a left-hander. He holds the sling he used to kill the giant Goliath in his left hand.

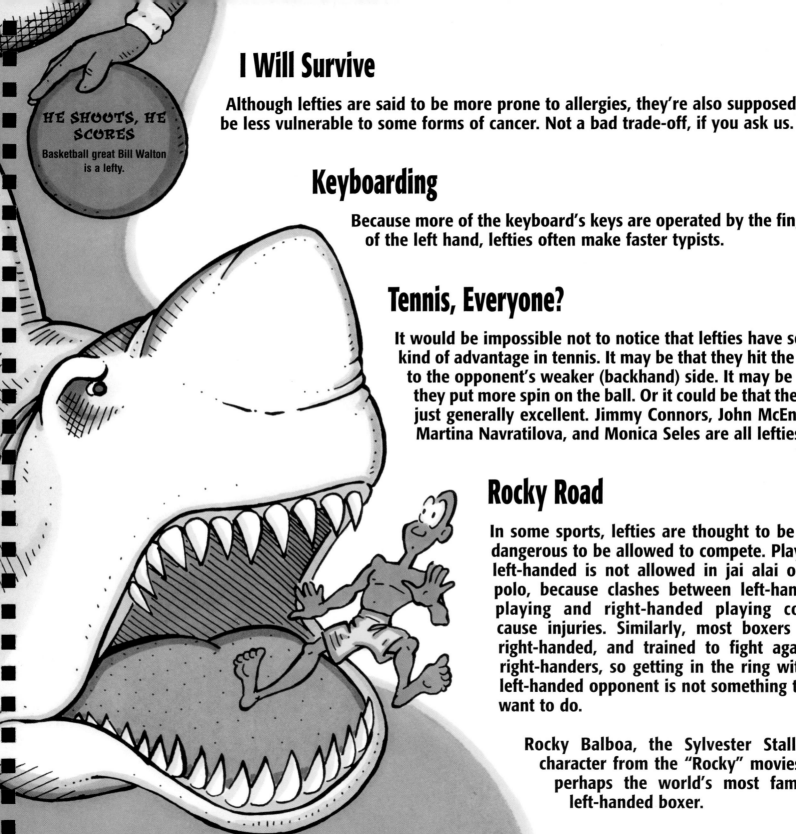

I Will Survive

Although lefties are said to be more prone to allergies, they're also supposed to be less vulnerable to some forms of cancer. Not a bad trade-off, if you ask us.

Keyboarding

Because more of the keyboard's keys are operated by the fingers of the left hand, lefties often make faster typists.

Tennis, Everyone?

It would be impossible not to notice that lefties have some kind of advantage in tennis. It may be that they hit the ball to the opponent's weaker (backhand) side. It may be that they put more spin on the ball. Or it could be that they're just generally excellent. Jimmy Connors, John McEnroe, Martina Navratilova, and Monica Seles are all lefties.

Rocky Road

In some sports, lefties are thought to be too dangerous to be allowed to compete. Playing left-handed is not allowed in jai alai or in polo, because clashes between left-handed playing and right-handed playing could cause injuries. Similarly, most boxers are right-handed, and trained to fight against right-handers, so getting in the ring with a left-handed opponent is not something they want to do.

Rocky Balboa, the Sylvester Stallone character from the "Rocky" movies, is perhaps the world's most famous left-handed boxer.

HE SHOOTS, HE SCORES
Basketball great Bill Walton is a lefty.

Shake It Up
HOW TO FREAK SOMEONE OUT

The next time someone tries to shake hands with you, instead of offering your right hand, offer your left. You'll cause major confusion. Why is this? Why do left-handed people have to offer their right hand for a handshake? A better question might be why we shake hands at all. It's a strange custom, when you think about it. Kind of germy, too, considering that most people sneeze and cough into their hands. "Hello, there. Nice to meet you. Allow me to hand you some germs."

But there's really no getting around handshaking. It's one of the oldest gestures in the world. If you went back to ancient Greece, you'd see people shaking hands. And if you visited ancient Rome, you'd see something even more bizarre: people shaking hands with statues of the gods. Slipping the gods some skin was considered good luck.

"Yo, Jupiter. 'Sup?"

As for why we have to offer our right hands, you won't believe the answer. Way back when people were a tad more violent than they are now, they often carried knives and other weapons. If you met someone, you'd try to shake his hand so that you could make sure he wasn't carrying a dagger in it. He'd want to know the same thing about you. You'd shake right hands because most people are right-handed, so you've got the greatest odds of seeing the hand that would hold the weapon.

One theory holds that left-handed people developed a reputation for being untrustworthy and dangerous because they were able to shake hands with their right hands and still conceal a knife in their strong left hand.

So, basically, they were considered dangerous simply for being . . . handy.

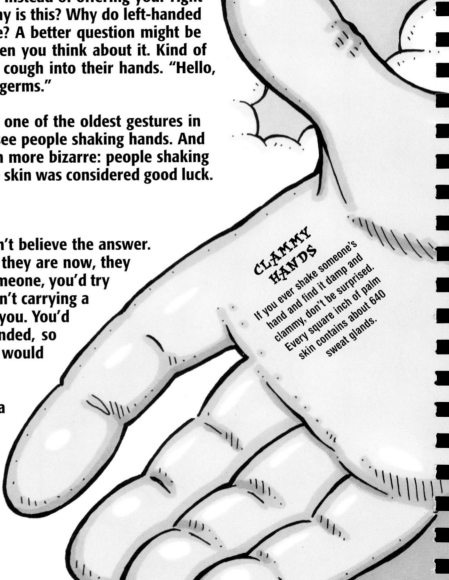

CLAMMY HANDS
If you ever shake someone's hand and find it damp and clammy, don't be surprised. Every square inch of palm skin contains about 640 sweat glands.

SHAKE AND BREAK

President Theodore Roosevelt broke the record for number of hands shaken by a public figure at an official function when he shook 8,513 hands on New Year's Day, 1907, at the White House.

47

The Brave Lefty Shake

HOWDY, BOYS

There is at least one exception to the you-must-shake-with-your-right-hand rule. But if you're a girl, forget it. It's the handshake of the Boy Scouts of America.

The guy who founded the Boy Scouts, Lord Robert Baden-Powell, was ambidextrous. Apparently, though, that's not why he decided that the Boy Scout shake should be left-handed.

Once, when he was visiting Africa, he heard about two neighboring societies who were always fighting each other. Baden-Powell was told that one of the chiefs of the societies made peace with the chief of the other society by putting his weapon down and walking toward him with his left hand extended.

From that time on, the bravest warriors of the tribe greeted each other with the left-handed handshake, because it was considered a sign of trust, and because the left hand was thought to be especially important due to its being nearer to the heart.

CRUSHING WEIGHT

The average handshake (from an adult) exerts 90 pounds of pressure. Ninety pounds! Someone who's really squashing your paw can put 150 pounds of pressure on it. Let's say that every person who shook President Roosevelt's hand on New Year's Day 1907 exerted 90 pounds of pressure on his hand. That makes 766,170 pounds of pressure! It's a wonder he ever shook again.

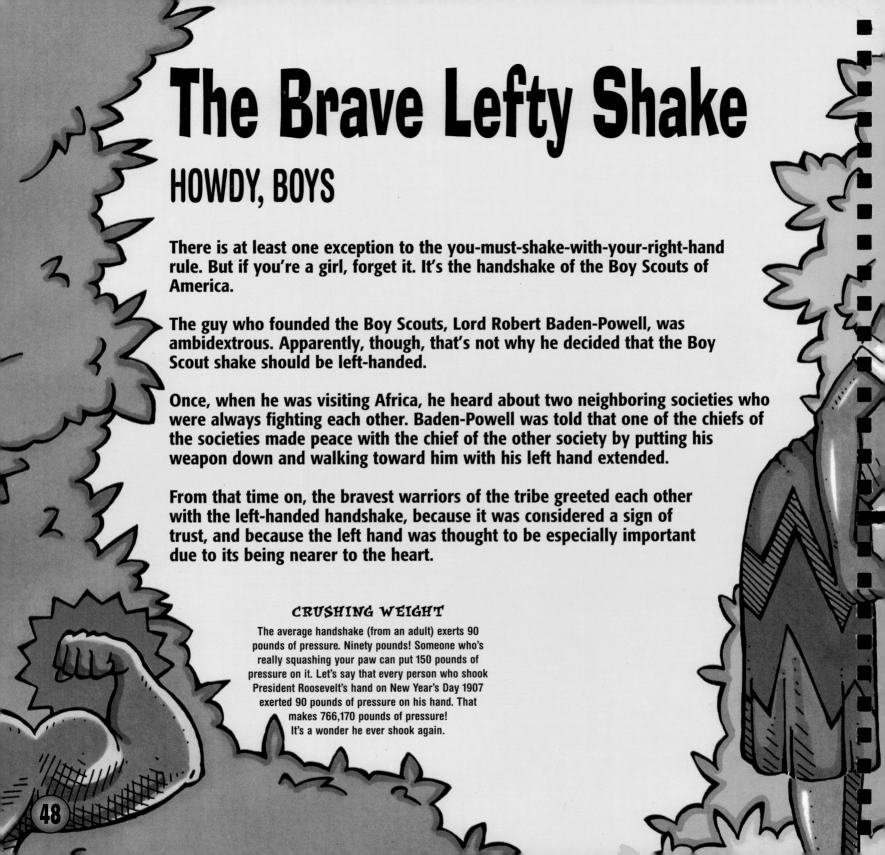

SMARTY HANDSHAKE

If you really work your tail off in college, you might get to be in a smart-person's club called Phi Beta Kappa. And if you get to be in that club, the Phi Beta Kappa people will teach you a secret (right-handed) handshake. Some of the Editors of Planet Dexter learned the Phi Beta Kappa handshake in college, but they've since completely forgotten what it was! Does that mean they aren't actually smart after all???

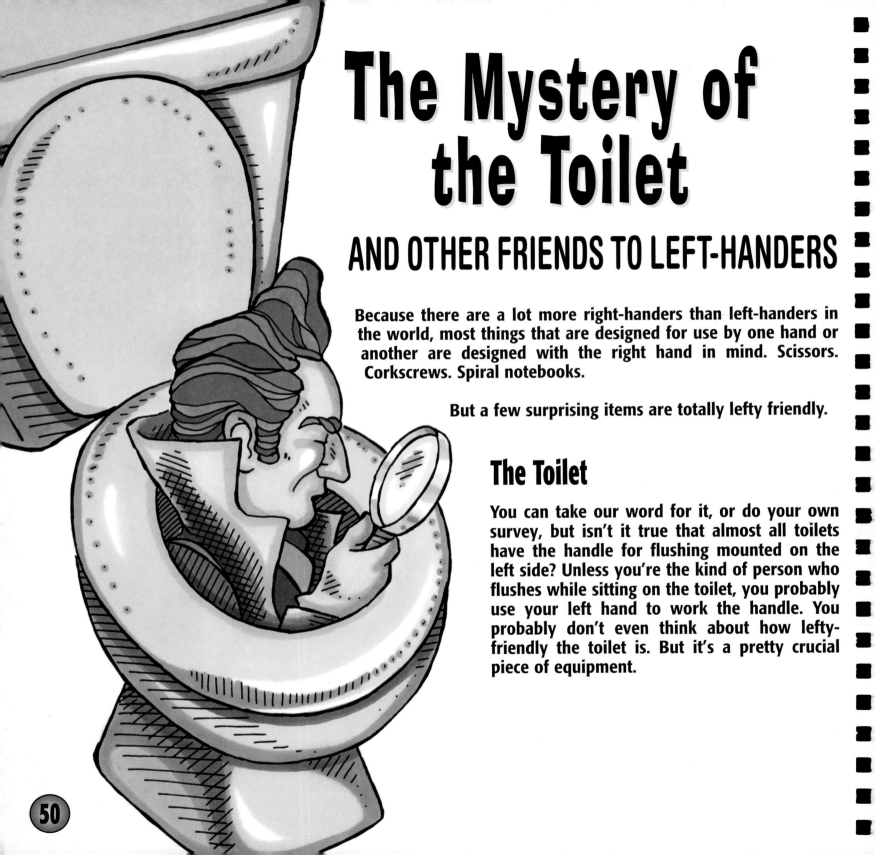

The Mystery of the Toilet

AND OTHER FRIENDS TO LEFT-HANDERS

Because there are a lot more right-handers than left-handers in the world, most things that are designed for use by one hand or another are designed with the right hand in mind. Scissors. Corkscrews. Spiral notebooks.

But a few surprising items are totally lefty friendly.

The Toilet

You can take our word for it, or do your own survey, but isn't it true that almost all toilets have the handle for flushing mounted on the left side? Unless you're the kind of person who flushes while sitting on the toilet, you probably use your left hand to work the handle. You probably don't even think about how lefty-friendly the toilet is. But it's a pretty crucial piece of equipment.

Car Stuff

Car stuff is kind of a mixed bag. If you have the kind of car with a gear shift, the gear shift is on the right-handed side. Fiddling with the radio or air conditioner, likewise, requires a right hand (unless you're the passenger of course).

But let's say you drive a car past a tollbooth. Or you go to McDonald's and decide to use the drive-through window. Or you go to a drive-through bank or ATM. In these cases, it's the left-handed side all the way.

In Great Britain, where the steering wheels are on the right side and cars are driven on the left side of the road, a lefty would deal with the reverse of the above situations.

The Sewing Machine

You might be sitting around naked or shabbily clothed this very second if it weren't for Elias Howe, the man who invented the sewing machine. It just so happens that Howe was left-handed, so he put the needle on the left side of the machine. There it has stayed to this day.

Babies

Really weird but true: if you hand a woman a baby, she'll almost always cradle the baby in her left arm. It doesn't matter if she's left-handed or right-handed. In fact, it doesn't even matter if she's human. Female gorillas, orangutans, and chimpanzees cradle their babies in their left arms, too.

Why??? No one knows.

One theory is that it's the right side of the brain that figures out emotional signals (like whether the baby is happy or sad or hungry or angry) and women may "know," without really thinking about it, that it's better to have the baby's head nearer to her left eye and ear, because stuff that goes in the left eye and ear goes right to the right side of the brain (see page 26).

But that doesn't explain why men don't seem to care which arm they hold babies in.

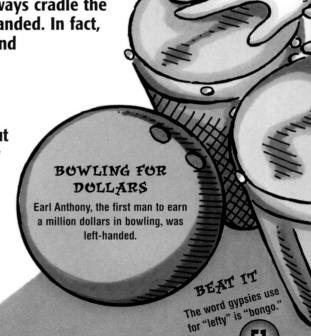

BOWLING FOR DOLLARS
Earl Anthony, the first man to earn a million dollars in bowling, was left-handed.

BEAT IT
The word gypsies use for "lefty" is "bongo."

Test Your Home

for Signs of Lefty Life

A CHECKLIST

TURN BACK TIME

Some of the first clocks had hands that ran not clockwise (to the right) but counterclockwise (to the left).

Is your home a friendly place for a lefty to live, or should you set about making some changes? Here's a list of things to look for. The more L's, the better.

1. When you stand facing a closet, is the front part of each garment on each clothes hanger facing the left side of the closet or the right?

❏ **L**   ❏ **R**

2. If you have a home computer with a mouse, on which side of the keyboard is the mouse resting?

❏ **L**   ❏ **R**

3. Go find a loaf of bread or other food item that's been secured in a bag with a twist tie. Is the twist turned to the left or to the right?

❏ **L**   ❏ **R**

4. While you're in the kitchen, check out a box of cereal. If the back of the box is facing you, on which side of the box is the inner liner torn open?

❏ **L**   ❏ **R**

5. When you're facing your front door from outside your home, is your doorbell on your left or your right?

❏ **L**   ❏ **R**

6. Go to a sink. Is the soap located on your left or your right?

❏ **L**   ❏ **R**

7. Are most of the light switches in your house located on your left side as you enter a room or on your right?

❏ **L**   ❏ **R**

8. Which way do the front covers of the books in your bookshelves face?

❏ **L**   ❏ **R**

9. If you're sitting on your toilet, on which side of you is the toilet paper dispenser?

❏ **L**   ❏ **R**

10. On which side of the bed do you get out in the morning?

❏ **L**   ❏ **R**

Scoring:

0 – 3 L's: Your home needs a little leftifying.
4 – 7 L's: Pretty good, but some improvements left to be made.
8 – 10 L's: Your home's a lefty paradise.

CHECK, PLEASE
Some companies make checkbooks for lefties, in which the checks tear off of a stub at the right-hand side.

To Hook or Not to Hook

READ SOMEONE'S MIND

If you're a lefty, there's a good chance that you're also a hooker.
A hooker, that is, as in "one who 'hooks' his or her hand when writing."

You know: when you write, you may bend your wrist, and hold the pencil so it points toward the bottom of the paper. That's "hooking." You might not do it. Some lefties do, some don't.

"Hooking" is much more common in left-handers than in right-handers; it's a pretty rare right-hander who hooks when writing. Lefties often say they hook because it's the only comfortable way to move their pen across the paper, especially when using spiral notebooks.

But at least one scientist believes that whether you hook or don't hook can tell you in what brain hemisphere your language skills are located. Here's the formula:

Lefty who hooks hand = Language center located in left half of brain

Lefty who doesn't hook = Language center located in right half of brain

Righty who hooks hand = Language center located in right half of brain

Righty who doesn't hook = Language center located in left half of brain

It's sorta neat to be able to look at the way someone is writing and guess something about the inside of that person's head. But this theory might not be totally true, so don't bet your life savings on it.

DIM BULB
Even the smartest people have brains that use about the same amount of energy needed to light a 10-watt light bulb.

CHECKMATE
Lefties are often naturally talented at chess.

55

I Want My LefTV!

A BRILLIANT LEFTY ONCE SAID, "I WANT MY LEFTV!"

She could have meant any number of things, but our best guess is that she wanted a whole channel devoted to lefties, 24 hours a day.

Turns out, her request wasn't so unreasonable. Many TV shows you watch are, in a way, LefTV already. For proof, tune in to the following chart:

THE SHOW	LEFTY ACTOR	CHARACTER
"The Nanny"	Fran Drescher	Fran Fine, a.k.a. the nanny
"Dave's World"	Harry Anderson	Dave Barry
"Seinfeld"	Jerry Seinfeld	Jerry Seinfeld
"Seinfeld"	Jason Alexander	George Costanza
"Seinfeld"	Michael Richards	Cosmo Kramer
"Home Improvement"	Tim Allen	Tim "The Tool Man" Taylor
"Beverly Hills 90210"	Luke Perry	Dylan McKay
"The Dick Van Dyke Show"	Dick Van Dyke	Rob Petrie
"Friends"	Lisa Kudrow	Phoebe Buffay
"ER"	Juliana Margulies	Nurse Carol Hathaway
"ER"	Sherry Stringfield	Doctor Susan Lewis
"Welcome Back Kotter"	Gabe Kaplan	Gabe Kotter
"The Mary Tyler Moore Show"	Cloris Leachman	Phyllis Lindstrom
"The Partridge Family"	Shirley Jones	Shirley Partridge, a.k.a. Mom
"Full House"	Mary-Kate Olsen	Michelle Tanner
"Mad About You"	Anne Ramsay	Lisa Stemple, a.k.a. Jamie's sister

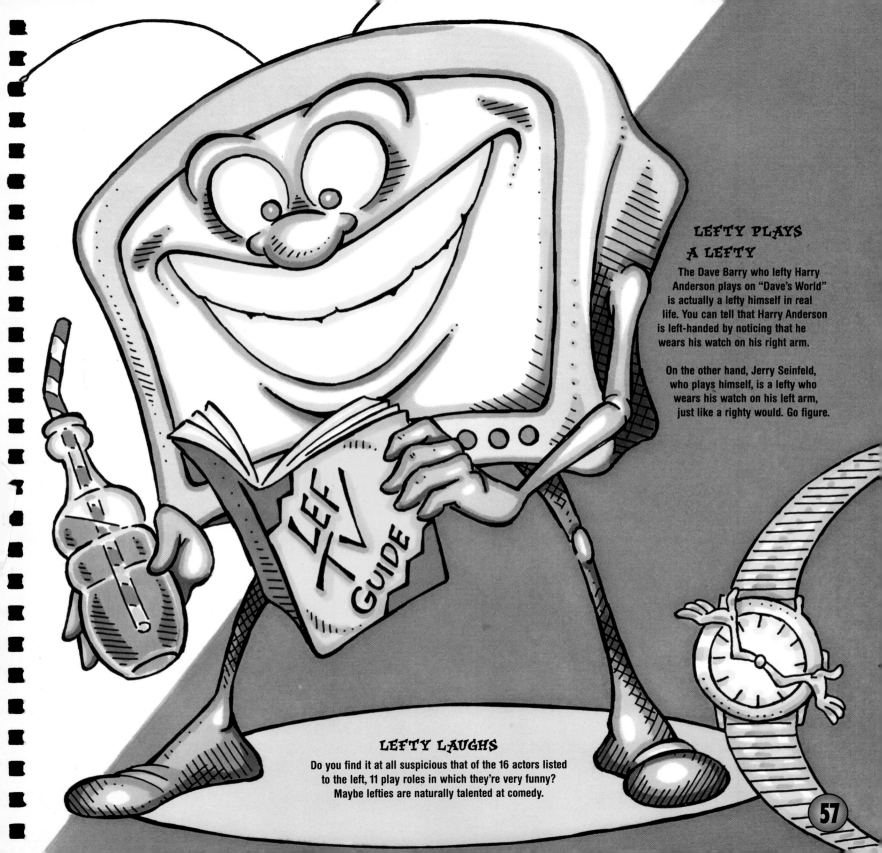

LEFTY PLAYS A LEFTY

The Dave Barry who lefty Harry Anderson plays on "Dave's World" is actually a lefty himself in real life. You can tell that Harry Anderson is left-handed by noticing that he wears his watch on his right arm.

On the other hand, Jerry Seinfeld, who plays himself, is a lefty who wears his watch on his left arm, just like a righty would. Go figure.

LEFTY LAUGHS

Do you find it at all suspicious that of the 16 actors listed to the left, 11 play roles in which they're very funny? Maybe lefties are naturally talented at comedy.

Lefty Lingo

Here are some ways we can all improve our language by removing negative phrases associated with "left," as well as positive phrases associated with "right."

INSTEAD OF SAYING . . .

"You're right!"

"Leftovers, again?"

"Righteous!"

"Are you in your right mind?"

"He's my right-hand man."

"Right on!"

"I'm still looking for Mr./Ms. Right."

"She's really out in left field with that idea."

"Might makes right!"

"That was a left-handed compliment if I've ever heard one."

"Dance with him at your own risk. He's got two left feet."

BUT WHY "PAW"?

The term "southpaw" was invented by Chicago Herald sportswriter Charles Seymour, who noticed that left-handed pitchers threw from the south side of the mound in Chicago's 1890 ballpark.

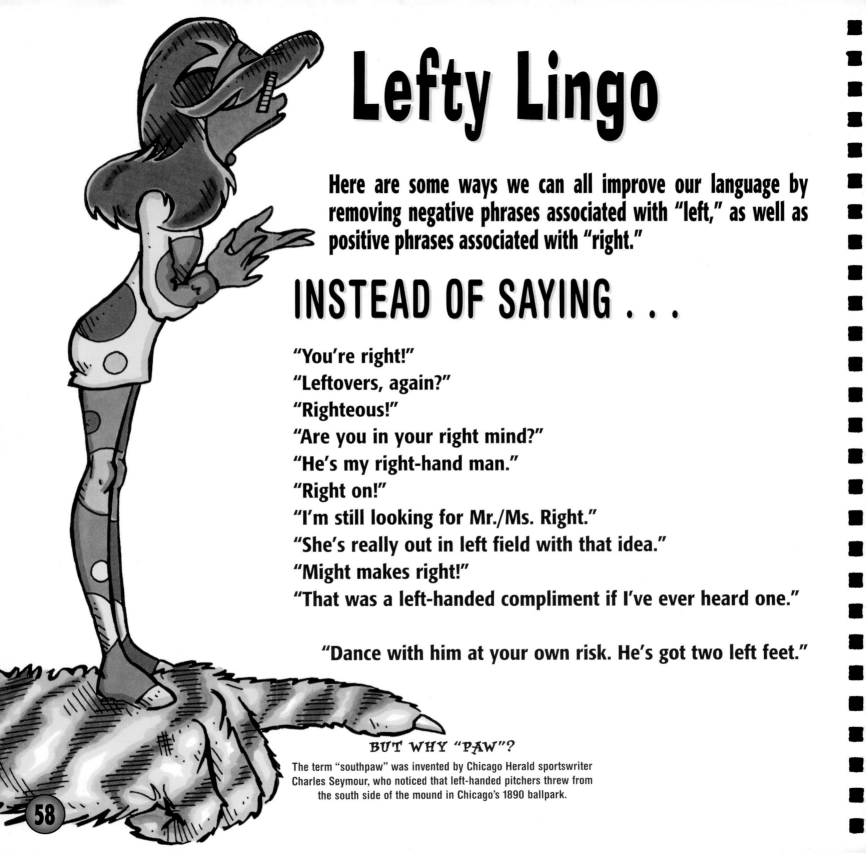

. . . SAY

"You're correct!"

"Used food, again?"

"Cool!"

"Are you sane?"

"He's my reliable bud."

"You go, girl!"

"I'm still looking for my soulmate."

"She's lost in space with that idea."

"Here's to brute force!"

"That was a pretty rotten thing to say, even though it sounded almost okay at first."

"Dance with him at your own risk. He's no twinkle-toes."

A NEW ONE

Australians sometimes call lefties "molly-dukers," which makes "southpaw" sound really normal.

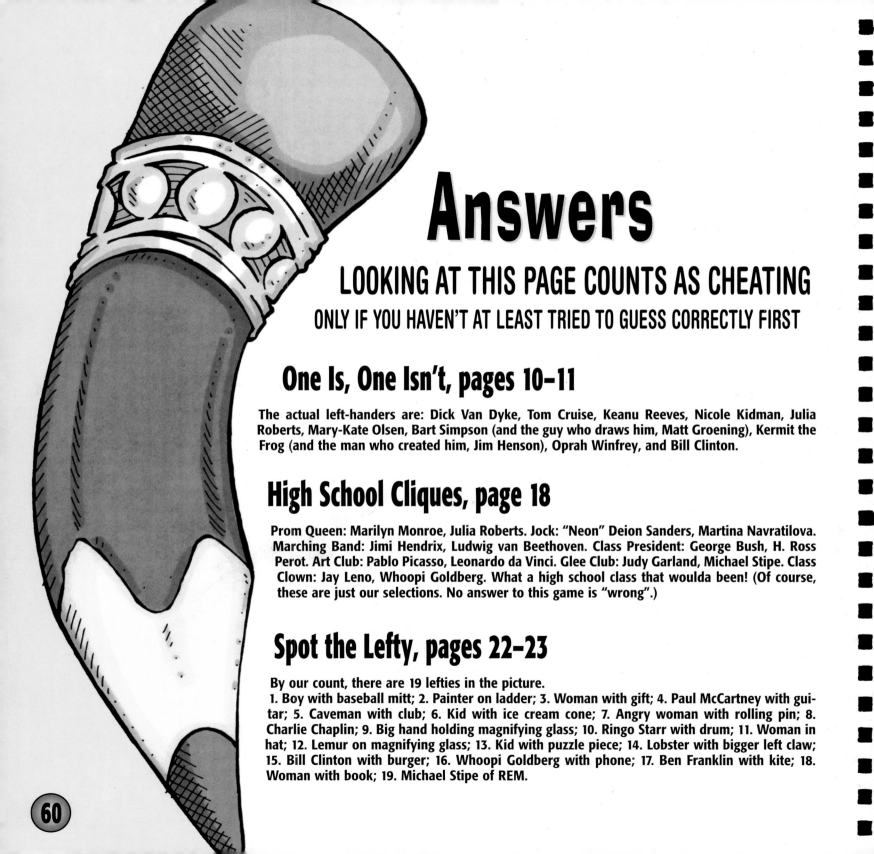

Answers

LOOKING AT THIS PAGE COUNTS AS CHEATING
ONLY IF YOU HAVEN'T AT LEAST TRIED TO GUESS CORRECTLY FIRST

One Is, One Isn't, pages 10–11

The actual left-handers are: Dick Van Dyke, Tom Cruise, Keanu Reeves, Nicole Kidman, Julia Roberts, Mary-Kate Olsen, Bart Simpson (and the guy who draws him, Matt Groening), Kermit the Frog (and the man who created him, Jim Henson), Oprah Winfrey, and Bill Clinton.

High School Cliques, page 18

Prom Queen: Marilyn Monroe, Julia Roberts. Jock: "Neon" Deion Sanders, Martina Navratilova. Marching Band: Jimi Hendrix, Ludwig van Beethoven. Class President: George Bush, H. Ross Perot. Art Club: Pablo Picasso, Leonardo da Vinci. Glee Club: Judy Garland, Michael Stipe. Class Clown: Jay Leno, Whoopi Goldberg. What a high school class that woulda been! (Of course, these are just our selections. No answer to this game is "wrong".)

Spot the Lefty, pages 22–23

By our count, there are 19 lefties in the picture.
1. Boy with baseball mitt; 2. Painter on ladder; 3. Woman with gift; 4. Paul McCartney with guitar; 5. Caveman with club; 6. Kid with ice cream cone; 7. Angry woman with rolling pin; 8. Charlie Chaplin; 9. Big hand holding magnifying glass; 10. Ringo Starr with drum; 11. Woman in hat; 12. Lemur on magnifying glass; 13. Kid with puzzle piece; 14. Lobster with bigger left claw; 15. Bill Clinton with burger; 16. Whoopi Goldberg with phone; 17. Ben Franklin with kite; 18. Woman with book; 19. Michael Stipe of REM.

Mad Scientist Stuff, pages 24-25

The bogus theories are The Smelly Theory and The Genius Theory, although many smart kids may indeed find being left-handed more interesting than being right-handed.

When Lefties Ruled, pages 34-35

1. c.
2. a. When left-handers draw things in profile, they almost always have the profile facing to the right. Right-handers draw it facing to the left.
3. d. Before sturdy tools could be made with bronze, everyone could make his or her own tools, and make those tools left-handed or right-handed. Once the tools were made to last, however, and were passed down through generations, it became a problem for people not to all have the same favorite hand. Or so some scientists believe, stating that the desire to use right-handed tools may have caused some lefties to "switch" to right-handedness.
4. a. Some other people think that people became mostly right-handed because, when they fought other people or animals, they fought with their right arm, while trying to protect their heart with their left arm, since the heart is on the left side.
5. b.
6. c.

Weird About Hands, pages 36-37

1. c; 2. b; 3. d; 4. d; 5. b; 6. a; 7. d.

The Bummer Pages, pages 40-41

So far as we know, nobody has ever said that lefties have a serious body odor problem, that they spend money on useless appliances, or that they tend to buy shoes in the wrong size. All of the rest of the statements on The Bummer Pages are extracted from books and studies about left-handers, though. Even the weird thing about the safecrackers. Keep in mind whenever you see some new or old "finding" about left-handers that lefties are a minority, and the majority (righties) love to pretend that there might be something better about being a majority than a minority.

What's Left to Say?

A FOND FAREWELL, NOW THAT YOU'VE REACHED THE "BEGINNING" OF THIS BOOK

Here on Planet Sinister, we publish books, not big ol' fat encyclopedias you can't carry around without straining some important muscle that'll stunt your growth forever.

So it's just about time to bring this book to a close.
But before we wave good-bye (with our left hands, of course!), here are a few really really bad jokes.
Read them, and you won't mind having to put this book aside.

What do you call a goose who favors his left wing?
Answer: A left-gander.

What do you call a southpaw rodeo worker?
Answer: A left-brander.

What would you call the left-handed lead singer of REM if he turned to a life of crime?
Answer: Michael Swipe.

What would you call Mary Tyler Moore's most famous left-handed co-star if he forgot how to ride a bike?
Answer: Dick Van Trike.

What do you call a right-handed baseball player?
Answer: Unfortunate.

More Strange Books

FROM PLANET DEXTER (A.K.A. PLANET SINISTER)

ANIMAL GROSSOLOGY™
The Science of All Creatures Gross and Disgusting
by Sylvia Branzei

The author of Planet Dexter's best-selling *Grossology* returns, with this often stomach-turning book about animal life. Find out how a fly eats (yikes!), how to learn from an owl pellet, why a hagfish is so slimy, what the deal is with leeches, and much more.

THE HAIRY BOOK
The (Uncut) Truth About the Weirdness of Hair
by The Editors of Planet Dexter

Think you know hair? Think again! This hair-covered book gives you the real scoop on everything from blue-haired dogs to werewolves, wacky styles, and hairy babies. Includes a truly stylin' comb for proper book grooming.

WHADDAYA DOIN' IN THERE?
A Bathroom Companion (for Kids!)
by The Editors of Planet Dexter

All smart kids read in the bathroom. But what to read? Answer: This book, if you can! *Whaddaya Doin' In There?* offers humor, bathroom lore, ghost stories, weird laws, lotsa trivia, you name it. It's the perfect tome for your toilet time. And it comes with a pine-scented air freshener!

AHEM!
THIS IS THE LAST PAGE OF THIS BOOK, NOT THE FIRST. THAT'S CORRECT. TURN TO THE OTHER END OF THE BOOK IF YOU'RE LOOKING FOR THE FIRST PAGE. AND DON'T USE THE WORD "STUPID." WE CAN HEAR EVERYTHING YOU SAY, YOU KNOW. WE STICK LITTLE MICROPHONES IN ALL OF OUR BOOKS.

JUST KIDDING. BUT WE REALLY DID MAKE THIS BOOK OPEN WEIRD ON PURPOSE.
DIG IT.